Safe In Starry Arms

Written by Christie Lea ★ Art by Di

Tellwell Talent
www.tellwell.ca

ISBN
978-0-2288-1814-4 (Hardcover)
978-0-2288-1813-7 (Paperback)

For my lovely, brave boy.
My first born – Nicholas.

When Nic was small he was afraid of life
He could not calm his mind although he tried
He cried at night and woke alone and sad
He hugged himself and wanted Mom and Dad

He thought of all the monsters there might be
Of all the scary sights that he might see
Of all the stories told to him by friends
Where children wind up eaten in the end

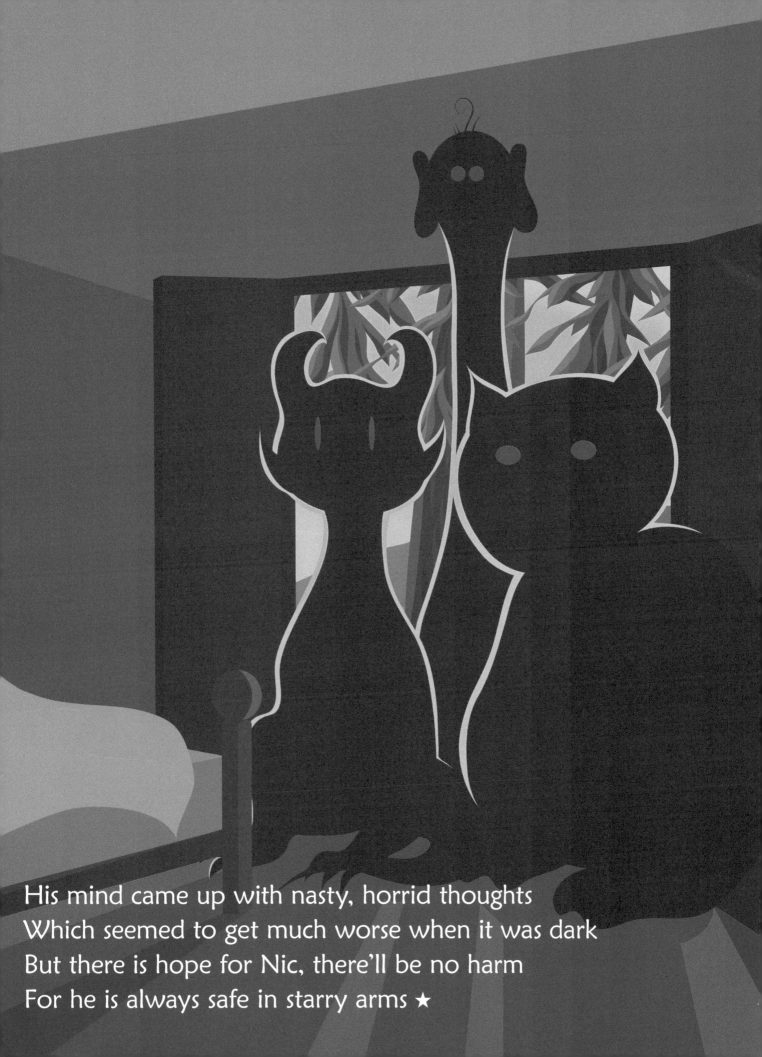

His mind came up with nasty, horrid thoughts
Which seemed to get much worse when it was dark
But there is hope for Nic, there'll be no harm
For he is always safe in starry arms ★

Nic is made up of mountains broad and high
He is the tips of trees that touch the sky
He is wide stumps so low and roots so deep
He is the stone beside the spruce who sleeps

He's peat, he's bog, he's mud, he's dirt, he's loam
Where seeds take root and call a place their home
And wait for water falling from the sky
To nourish shoots and send stalks climbing high

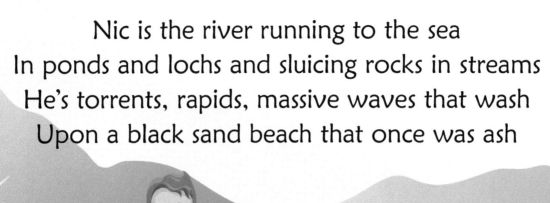

Nic is the river running to the sea
In ponds and lochs and sluicing rocks in streams
He's torrents, rapids, massive waves that wash
Upon a black sand beach that once was ash

The sea that blankets this blue Earth is Nic
Where orcas breach and tiny seahorse flit

Nic is the water sitting in a glass
With sunbeams dancing through it like a flash
Of lightning as it lunges from a cloud
Nic is the photon, carbon, and the sound

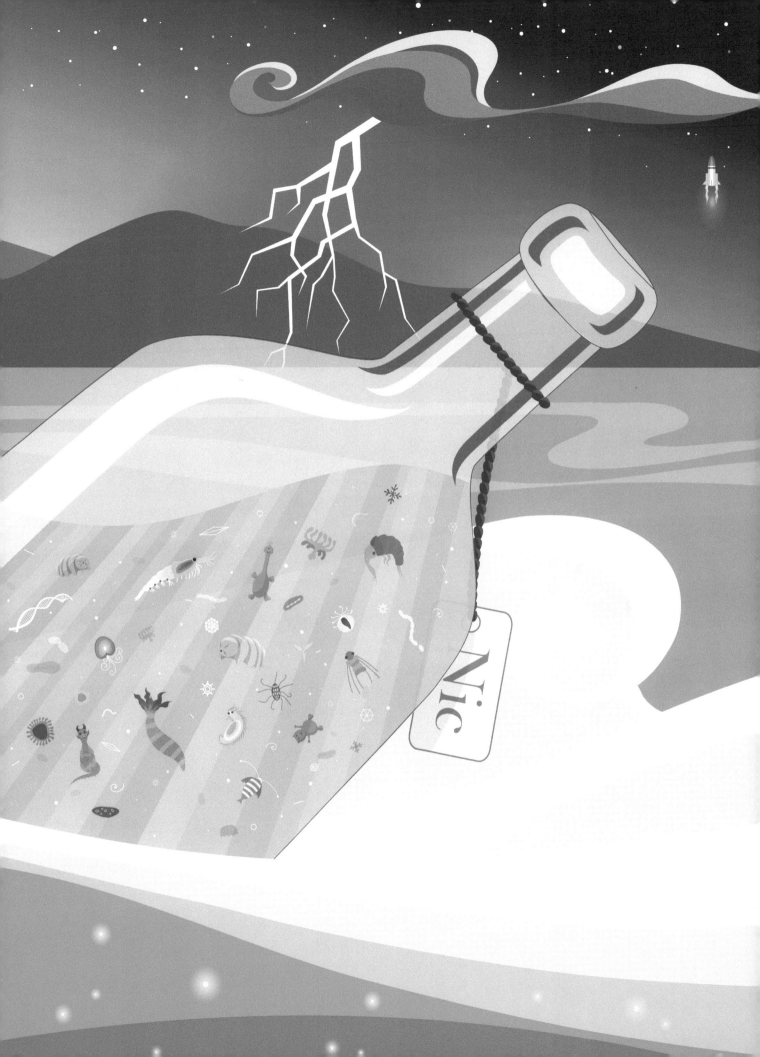

Of flames as they glow fiercely in the night
Nic is the shadows draped and shaped with light
The heat, the warmth, the fire under the ground
He is the molten furnace so far down

Nic is the atom splitting in our stars
He is the largest light source from afar
Our sun who washes planets with warm wind
Which kisses leaves and nurtures ev'rything

Nic is the air we breathe,
the breeze that blows
Soft on arms or slicing as it howls

He pushes clouds away over the peaks
And sends them back again in special shapes
Nic is the gust behind the mast and sail
Under the kite which chases its own tail

Nic is the tail that wags behind the dog
And is the soothing croaking of the frogs
Nic is the ant progressing up a hill
He is the slappy splashing of a seal

The silky regal wreath of lion's mane
The fish whose silver fins flash in the rain
Nic is the tear that slides down sister's cheek
Evaporating to a salty streak
The people perched upon his family tree
Who've helped him figure out that he is he

Nic is the calm beneath his troubled mind
Who's still and strong and present as he cries
The force who's somehow been there from the start
To fill his lungs and beat his little heart

Who never can be broken or afraid
Because he feels for certain that he's made

Of all things great and small
The wonder of it all
The beauty of this place
A mote in time and space
Of dancing lights above that blink their charm
Nic knows now that he's safe in starry arms ★

Lightning Source UK Ltd.
Milton Keynes UK
UKHW050327270121
377671UK00003B/144